PROMISES OF TOMORROW
VOLUME I

Inspirational Poems & Devotional Thoughts

McKINLEY COOPER, Jr.

PublishAmerica
Baltimore

First printing

ISBN: 1-4137-4021-9
PUBLISHED BY PUBLISHAMERICA, LLLP
www.publishamerica.com
Baltimore

Printed in the United States of America

This book is dedicated to the memory of my mother, Elizabeth Luckett Cooper. I first thank my Heavenly Father, who gave me all the inspiration I needed! To God be the glory for what He has done! "And ye now therefore have sorrow: but I will see you again, and your heart shall rejoice, and your joy, no man taketh from you" (John 16:22, KJV). I thank my wife, who read my writings first, and gave me her opinion on each and every one of them. I want to thank my daughter, who was inspired by her daddy spending so much time writing. I also thank my family and friends for inspiring me to help do God's work of spreading the good news. I truly thank everyone and give God all the glory! "My plan for you and everything I desire to do in your life is beyond what you could hope for; it is beyond what you could dream. I am able to do this as you put your trust in me and allow the power of my spirit to work within you" (Ephesians 3:20, AMP). Thank you, Lord. Amen

PROMISES OF TOMORROW

I think often about my memories of yesterday,
Those thoughts seem to slowly drift away.
You promised that you would be with me for a very long time,
Those memories are still in the back of my mind.
But I'm thinking about the most important promise you made to me,
That You will never leave me, nor forsake me, and set my life free.
You told me in "Your Word" that You would be there for me until the very end,
I truly thank You for making Jesus Christ my "real friend."
Why should you tell someone something that is not true,
But that's why I'm still left in this "Old World" feeling down and out and blue.
Try not to make promises that you aren't capable of keeping,
Then I won't be left here thinking about you and weeping.

WEEPING MAY ENDURE FOR A NIGHT,
BUT JOY WILL COME IN THE MORNING.

CONTENTS

Part Two

INTRODUCTION

These poems and devotional thoughts are inspirational to anyone who truly needs the Lord! They were designed to uplift the soul of anyone sinking into sin. They really inspired me to keep on doing God's will of bringing people closer to Him! I truly thank my Heavenly Father for putting His love and commandments into my heart and mind. I love the Lord with all my heart and soul! I pray that they may benefit someone who is going through some type of crisis right now! *Promises of Tomorrow* chronicles moments of my journey into the Christian environment through prayer and faith. It is not based upon my will, but God's will! Throughout the book, I will combine a personal observation with a spiritual interpretation in an effort to carve a place for Christianity in modern society.

The Lord is my rock, my fortress, and my deliverer, my God, my strength, in whom I will trust, my buckler, and the horn of my salvation, and my high tower. May God continue to bless each and everyone! AMEN.

PART ONE

THE POWER OF PRAYER

Prayer is a powerful weapon against evil in today's society. Whatever you are going through or about to go through, ask the Lord to give you the strength to endure to the end! It is better to have and not need, than to need and don't have. When Moses prayed to God to deliver the slaves of Egypt out of bondage, his prayer to God parted the Red Sea. Prayer has kept us from hurt, harm, and danger because God is always in the midst! All we have to do is to acknowledge that it wasn't our will! Prayer is our communication with God, because we can't call Him on the telephone, pager, fax, or e-mail Him. "And I say unto you, ask and it shall be given; seek and ye shall find; knock and it shall be opened unto you" (Luke 11:9, KJV).

How do you think God will know what your heart desire is, if you don't go to Him in prayer? Prayer can move mountains, control the winds and the rains, tame wild animals, raise the dead, heal your body, etc. We should go to God in prayer, not only in the bad times, but also during the good times! Some of us only pray to God when we want something. We need to pray both in and out of seasons! Sometimes we're too busy that we don't have time to pray!

Now, what if God was too busy to answer our prayers? "And this is the confidence that we have in Him, that if we ask anything according to His will, He hearth us: And if we know that He hear us, whatsoever we ask, we know that we have the petitions that we desired of Him" (I John 5: 14-15, KJV).

Prayer of the righteous will be answered! We must have faith and believe that whatever we ask the Lord for, He'll give it to us! I thank God for answering all my prayers, both past and present. Thank God. Amen.

GOD WILL MAKE A WAY

When you feel that all your hope is gone,
Don't give up, God will never leave you alone.
You may feel like giving up,
Put your trust in the Lord, He'll give you back your luck!
I love the Lord with all my heart,
He's been there for me from the very start!
Sometimes I sit and wonder, why He loves me so,
Even when my soul was down under.
When you're faced with problems, don't try to run away,
God will make a way out of no way!
You might think that you are trapped in sin,
He'll renew your life, so you can start all over again.
So when you feel left out, disgusted, and depressed,
Remember, God is always there to deliver you from stress!

I THANK GOD

One thing I have come to realize on my Christian journey is that God is always in the blessing business! He may not come when you want Him to, but He always show up in the nick of time! He has no favors or picks when it comes to loving Him! On the other hand, man only sees the outside and not the inside of us. God treats all of His children the same. I truly thank Him daily for giving me another chance on life! I could have been dead, sleeping in my grave, but He wasn't quite through with me yet! I just can't ever thank Him enough! He is good all the time! I have promised Him that I will do His will until the day I die!

One day, I hope to meet Him and tell Him how much I love Him! I've come this far by faith, and I know one day that faith will lead me home! I thank God for being there for me when I really needed Him.

"For God so loved the world that He gave His only begotten Son, that whosoever believeth in Him should not perish but have everlasting life" (John 3:16, KJV).

MAY GOD CONTINUE TO BLESS US! AMERICA, BLESS GOD!

WHO GOD IS TO ME

No matter what you accomplish or try to do,
God is always there for you!
When you try to do things on your own,
He's there to show you what you did wrong!
Whatever you do, put Him first in your life,
Pray to God to make things right!
I know one day my life will end,
It will be so good to see my best friend.
Sometimes I feel like I am in the movie *Left Behind*,
But I know God is always on time!
He makes me happy when I feel sad,
He puts joy in my heart and makes me glad!
I know He will never leave me alone,
One day I will be called on "Home."
God means a whole lot to me,
He protects me and set my life free.
He's my sword, shield, and ruler of all,
If I need anything, all I have to do is call.

FAITHFULNESS

When I think about being faithful, I think about "Old Job." He was faithful to God, no matter what trials or tribulations he was faced with! He lost everything that he had, but he still loved God! He didn't just sit around and feel sorry for himself, but he praised God *anyhow!* It takes a strong man to withstand all these tests of faith! You know, everybody talked about him, even his wife. They said that he should curse God and die! But, I like "Old Job," he didn't give up! After everything that he went through, God gave him back everything that he had lost!

This story even exists in today's times. God will open up the windows and pour you out blessings that you won't have room enough to receive! "Do not let go of the hope you cherish and confess. Seize it and hold it tight. Put your hope in what I have promised you for I am reliable, trustworthy, and faithful to my word" (Hebrews 10:23, AMP).

Man perishes every day because of lack of knowledge about God! You know it's hard to be like Job, because he truly kept the faith! Just imagine if this happened to you, could you endure to the end? Would you give up? What would you do in this situation? One thing I know is that you must have trust in God and put it all in His hands! I know that He has all power, both in Heaven and on Earth!

"Faith is the substance of things hoped for and the evidence of the things not seen." No matter what tragedies we may encounter in life, we must keep the faith! "His Lord said unto him, well done, good and faithful servant; thou hast been faithful over a few things, I will make thee ruler over many things; enter thou into the joy of thy Lord" Matthew 25:23, KJV). I pray that the Lord will keep me faithful through all the trials and tribulations I'm going through right now! Thank God. Amen.

THESE TRIALS AND TESTS OF FAITH
WILL ONLY MAKE ME STRONG!

LOVE LIFTED ME

From deep within the depths of sin,
God lifted me up and a new life begin!
I wondered why he loved me so,
He said, "Son, how much, you'll never know!"
I felt like Job, I've lost everything,
But from the depths of sin, new life begins!
God gave His Son's life to save me,
I know Heaven is where I want to be!
No more tears, except tears of joy,
I've longed for God's love since I was a boy.
I'll be united with my loved ones who I grieve,
When I see them again, my heart will be pleased!
Thank you Lord for lifting me up,
I can take all my tears and fill up a cup.
I love the Lord with all my heart,
I thank Him daily for a brand new start!

COMMITMENT

When I got married, I made a commitment to God and my wife to love and cherish her until death do us part! Well, after thirteen years, my commitment still stands strong! On April 15, 2002, my life almost came to an end! But by me making a serious commitment to God to serve Him until the end, I'm still here! I truly thank God for sparing my life and for giving me another chance! I am truly committed!

Now, this reminds me of a story I was told a long time ago. There was a man on a hill with a cage full of birds. He was torturing the birds one by one as he took them out of the cage. By this time, a young man came walking by and saw what was happening. The young man asked the man what would he take for the birds. The man told the young man that they weren't worth much, just give him a dollar. The young man took the birds and opened the door. He told the birds that they were free, because he had paid the price! The birds were afraid because they didn't know if they could trust the young man. After a while the birds flew away.

Then I'm reminded of when Jesus came in contact with the devil. The devil told Jesus that in order for Him to set man free that he would sacrifice his life. The devil told Jesus that man was "no good." The devil said that he would just fill man up with the "World" and just kill him. There were adulterers, whore-mongers, idolaters, and other sinful people out there! Jesus agreed to die for man's sin. He told man that he was free, because "I have paid the price." "There is no greater love than when a man would lay down his life for a friend! I thank you, Jesus, for the commitment you made to us! "For God so loved the world that He gave His only begotten Son, that whosoever believe upon Him shall not perish, but have eternal life" (John 3:16, KJV).

When you put your confidence in men, it sometimes fades away because of something said or done, but your commitment to God stands strong! "Blessed are those who do His commandments, that they have the right to the tree of life (Revelation 22:14, KJV). Thank God. Amen.

ARE YOU TRULY COMMITTED?

DON'T GIVE UP

When your troubles and trials have gotten you down,
Don't give up, because God is always somewhere around!
He knows when you walk, talk, or sit,
If you truly believe in Him, you'll never quit!
You may be stuck in a situation and there seems to be no way out,
A serious prayer to God will remove all your doubt!
Your friends may turn their backs on you.
The Lord will always bring you through!
Sometimes your situation may be so bad it makes you cry,
It hurts so much you may want to die.
But be patient, and hold on,
Your breakthrough may come, by someone on the telephone!

FORGIVENESS

It's easy to tell someone that you forgive them, but do you really mean it? You might not really know how that person feel about the situation, but God knows! If you truly believe in God, then there is forgiveness in your heart! You must treat your brothers and sisters with understanding; knowing their faults and weaknesses. If you are going through any trials and tribulations dealing with forgiveness, then pray to God to give you a forgiving heart! We should love our brothers and sisters "in spite of." Don't forget when Jesus died for your sins, He forgave you! Just think, we would all go to Hell right now, if God didn't forgive us! "And when ye stand praying, forgive, if ye have ought against any: that your Father also which is in Heaven may forgive you, your trespasses" (Mark 11:25-26).

We sometimes forget the teachings of the Bible on forgiveness. "For God said to forgive our trespassers as they trespass against us." We need to pray for those who despitefully use us. God has forgiven us of all our sins. I truly thank Him for forgiving me! "Let all bitterness, and wrath, and anger, and clamor, and evil speaking, be put away from you, with all malice: And be ye kind to one another, tenderhearted, forgiving one another, even as God for Christ's sake hath forgiven you" Ephesians 4:31-32, KJV). If someone would commit a sin against you or your family, could you truly forgive him? Only you know the real answer to the question! I pray that God will forgive me all of sins, both past and present! Thank God. Amen.

WHY CAN'T WE FORGIVE OUR BROTHERS?

WHAT A WONDERFUL LIFE

What a wonderful life this would be,
If we all could live in perfect harmony.
Why should we have to struggle?
When all we need to do is love our brother!
I think about this and it makes me sad,
That people could make me feel so bad.
Jesus died for all our sins,
Why do we have to mistreat our friends?
When I die I want to be buried deep,
Away from all of the hate and deceit!
When I was young I thought that all men were good,
I found out that "brotherly love" was only taught in Sunday school.
I pray to God to deliver me from sin,
Take my soul and make me whole again!
I try to live a life that is pleasing to Him,
If I don't change, I'll be just like the rest of them!
I'm going to take is easy and enjoy life,
The things I've done wrong, I'm going to make them right!

PEACE

With everything that is going on in the world today, I sometimes wonder, "Where can I go for peace?" It seems as if there is no peace anywhere on Earth! This country, the United States of America, has always been labeled a "peacekeeper." But how can you be keeping the peace when you are involved in a war? When you put all your trust in man: "He steals, kills, and destroys!" That's why we need to put all our trust in God! If you look on the back of money, you'll see "In God We Trust." Now, this is a true saying because we need to put all our trust in God! There seems to be no peace in your home, on the job, or in the church! The only peace you may have is when you go into prayer with God! A songwriter said that, "You Are My Peace and I Worship You." God is truly the only peace we have!

"Peace I leave with you, my peace I give unto you: not as the world giveth, give I unto you. Let not your heart be troubled, neither let it be afraid" (John 14:27, KJV).

We must learn to go to God for everything that man can't solve! God is "in charge" of everything that happens in our lives. Sometimes we have to go through some things just for Him to bring us out! I was once told as a young man that the only peace you get is when you die! I totally disagree with this comment. If you end up going to Hell, then you still won't have any peace!

My prayer is always for peace. "If it is possible, as much as lieth in you, live peaceably with all men" (Romans 12:18, KJV). I hope and pray that everyone on Earth could live together in peace! The hardest thing in the world for us to do is to get along with our brothers and sisters. We sometimes forget that Jesus loved us all in spite of all our sins! He took on all our weaknesses and downfalls just for us to live together in peace! Thank you, Jesus. Amen.

CAN'T WE ALL JUST GET ALONG?

GOING HOME

One day I'll make the greatest sacrifice,
I'll leave this old world and begin a brand-new life.
There will be no more heart-aches and pain,
No more storms and no more rain.
The peace I will have will last forever,
I thank God that I won't see anymore bad weather!
They say "home is where the heart is,"
I want to go where Jesus lives!
We will all leave this place one day,
And all go our separate ways.
Everyday, I hope and pray to go to a better place,
Sometimes I get tired of running this same old race!
It's something special being in the presence of the Lord,
When I go home, I'll be making a brand new start!

WORDS OF ENCOURAGEMENT

You need to first thank God for giving you the ability to do whatever you want to accomplish in life! As a young man or woman, you will face many encounters that will be a test of your faith. Peer pressure will be your number-one test! You are trying to make something of yourself, but some of your "so-called friends" will always make trouble for you. Always remember that God is everywhere! Just keep your thoughts on Him, no matter where you may be located. Put Him first in your life and sit back and enjoy the results.

Remember, the devil will do all he can to discourage you and make you give up. All you need to do is ask God for guidance and protection, and He will do just what He say He will do.

When it seems as though you don't have any friends, you have one in Jesus! He is your "real friend." One who has been there from the beginning, and will be there to the end. Just trust and believe in Him, He'll bring you out! When you get lonely, depressed, or angry, just have a talk with Him. Keep up your confidence in yourself, and don't worry about what other people may think about you. "I did not create you to be a failure. I created you to be a success. I have promised that if you will meditate in my word and walk in my ways, your life will be prosperous and successful" (Joshua 1:8).

P.S. GOD LOVES YOU!

LIFE GOES ON

You may be suffering form the lost of a loved one, who was very close,
God knows what's best and He loves us the most.
Everything happens for a reason,
It doesn't matter when or where, or during what season.
But don't give up; be strong,
Believe what God promises to you because life still goes on!
Think a lot about the life that you live,
Your dedication to Christ and the time you give.
Don't spend your whole life worrying about another,
You need to learn how to love and respect your brother!
If you go to Heaven, you'll be fine,
Because you left this old, "cruel world" at the right time!

A SPIRITUAL WARFARE

We as Christians, are fighting a spiritual warfare every day of our lives! It is a continuous battle in our churches over religion. God has given everyone gifts according to His will and purpose. We all have our own special talents in one area, not all the areas of teaching in the church. I was once told by one of my elders that "it's more Hell in the church than on the streets!"

God directs us another way, when everything bad seems to happen to you! Some people are making up their own churches, trying to get away from all the confusion that's going on in the traditional churches. A lot of other people just stay at home, and decide to not even go to church.

Remember, the devil wants us to be drawn away from the church, so he can keep us in the "world." We need to have a "worldwide revival" to bring the people back into our churches and back to the Lord! As for me, I will continue to bless the Lord and His name shall continuously be in my mouth at all times! We must take a good look at ourselves, both inside and outside. If we are lacking in some areas, ask the Lord for guidance! We need the Lord now, more than anything else.

One thing to remember is that "God Has Not Forgotten About You." He's still and always will be there! "Trust in the Lord with all thine heart; and lean not unto thy own understanding. In all thy ways acknowledge Him, and He shall direct thy paths" (Proverbs 3:5-6, KJV). "For God is not unrighteous to forget your work and labour of love, which ye have shewed toward His name, in that ye have ministered to the saints, and do minister" (Hebrews 6:10, KJV).

I thank God for fighting all my battles! Amen.

IF GOD BE FOR YOU,
THEN WHO IS THE WORLD AGAINST YOU?

DON'T LET LIFE PASS YOU BY

Sometimes you may feel like giving in,
But Jesus died to deliver you from sin.
Don't dwell in the past,
The things that happened to you will not last!
Concentrate on doing your very best,
Always remember that your trials are just a test!
God puts you through some things just to bring you out,
He lets you know not to worry or have any doubt.
Do things that is pleasing to the "One Above,"
Shower your friends and family with nothing but love!
So don't just sit around and let life pass you by,
Do something that is pleasing to the "One on High!"

MISSING YOU: A LETTER TO MY MOTHER

I sometimes sit and wonder, "What If?" God has a plan for each and everyone of us. But why should we feel so much pain when someone very close to us dies? You can quote scripture after scripture to me, but the pain never goes away! My heart is broken and it's very hard to mend it! But God knows what's in my heart, and makes it strong again!

The greatest pain I feel comes during the holidays! I thought that I would write you a letter to ease my pain. Sometimes when I think about you, I feel so alone. I miss you so much! I would like to tell you how I truly feel about you.

You were always my role model. You had the qualities of an angel; looking after everyone—your children, grandchildren, great-grandchildren, cousins, friends, etc. You always had an encouraging word to say about life to me at an early age. The time we spent fishing was educational to me! You told me the way that I should go and always to remember to keep God first in my life! I sometimes dream about those times, and I remember them like yesterday!

When I see you again, I would like to tell you, "Happy Valentine's Day;" "I Love You," "Happy Birthday;" "Happy Mother's Day to one of the best mothers in the world," "Happy Thanksgiving and I thank God for giving me such a wonderful mother!"

Christmas just ain't Christmas without the one you love! This is supposed to be the most joyful time of the year, but it doesn't seem like it to me. You always wanted the best for me, or nothing to happen to me. During this holiday season, I need to spend time with my Heavenly Father, who has taken your place right now. I just need to "Let go and to let God." I know that He will make everything all right.

Whenever I feel lonely and depressed, I need to have a talk with God. I know that the line is never too busy, and He will answer my prayers! The tears I shed will be tears of joy and not of sorrow. "My son, attend to my words;

consent to my saying. Let them not depart from your sight: keep them in the center of your heart. For they are life to those who find them, healing and health to all their flesh" (Proverbs 4:20-22).

What a blessing it was to share forty years of my life with you! God has touched my life in so many ways through the gift of your love! "Love is patient, love is kind…It always protects, always trusts, always hopes, always preserves. Love never fails…" (1 Corinthians 13:4,7-8).

I will always miss you, but I know we will see each other again "on that other shore." I love you very much! Thank God. Amen.

JESUS IS THE REASON FOR THE SEASON!

IT'S SO HARD TO SAY GOOD-BYE

It's so hard to say good-bye,
To the years that have passed us by.
Some made you laugh, some made you cry,
Some people will live, some will die!
But God is ever present in our world today,
Just put your trust in Him; He'll make a way!
You sometimes get caught up in a whole lot of mess,
It doesn't matter if you live in the north, south, east, or west.
Before you know it, your life is over and you're gone,
You find yourself facing God before His "Heavenly Throne!"
"What did I do wrong? Why am I here?"
God answers you and says, "That you were so dear!"
I took you away from your family and friends,
You now have a chance to live your life to the pleasant end!
You'll see your family and friends again,
To live in peace and be free from sin!
Live a life that is pleasing to the "One Above,"
So when you leave, you'll be remembered with nothing but love!

HEALING

Healing comes about through faith in God. I'm a true witness of God's healing power, because I was diagnosed with congestive heart failure on April 16, 2002. I'd never been sick enough to go to the hospital in forty years. I now lay on my back in the bed, looking up towards the ceiling. All I could do was to talk to God about healing my body. I prayed to God to heal my body. I also asked Him to forgive me of all my sins, and to make me whole again. Every test that was done on me at the hospital came up negative! Praise the Lord! The doctor couldn't tell me what was actually happening. He didn't even want to admit that I was experiencing a true "Miracle of God!" I just lay there, feeling the healing power of God! I know that I can do all things through Christ, who strengthens me! God had already told me that the doctor was put there to confirm my illness.

For I will restore health unto thee, and I will heal thee of thy wounds, saith the Lord; because they called thee an outcast, saying, "This in Zion, whom no man seeketh after" (Jeremiah 30:17, KJV). God had told me that everything would be all right, because I "believed" in Him. A friend of the family came by, and dropped me off some tapes on healing on our doorsteps. Now, just look at God's grace and mercy! I lay in my bed one morning and was ministered to by the radio. A lot of songs on healing played for about three to four hours, without a commercial break. I just cried, cried, and cried until I couldn't shed another tear. I could feel the power of healing spread throughout my body. Look to the hills from where cometh your strength, for your strength cometh from the Lord. I felt whole again! I praise His Holy name!

God told me that some will believe what I tell them, and some won't believe me, just as they did Jesus. I was reminded to read Psalm 118 whenever I needed to be reminded about what was actually happening in my life. I know that God didn't bring me this far to leave me. I know that He has plans for my life. All I need to do is put everything in His hands! Whatever He asks me to do, I must be obedient to His will and way. You know, our healing is in God's hands!

"I am the Lord that healeth thee" (Exodus 15:26, KJV).

I often think about the United States of America, my homeland. We are going through many trials and tribulations. God is our only defense against our enemies. He is all we have, and all we will ever need. Thank you, Lord. Amen.

I THANK YOU, LORD, FOR HEALING ME!

WHAT HAVE I DONE FOR GOD LATELY?

What can I do for someone who does so much for me?
He heals my body and enables me to see.
I praise and worship His holy name,
I thank Him daily for making my life change.
I could live a lifetime, but I can't thank Him enough,
He was right there for me when the going got rough.
What, may I ask, is a man to do?
God does all this for you, because He loves you.
I should climb up the highest mountain top and shout,
Just to let everyone know how God brought me out!
When my soul was sinking into sin,
He lifted me back up, to let a new life begin.
God has an awesome power,
He directs your path and all of His love is "showered."
I know He will deliver me one day from running this "old race."
To a holy and beautiful place!
Now, can you truly understand,
How to love and appreciate someone greater than man?

MONKEY SEE, MONKEY DO

Are you trying to keep up with the Joneses? Are you jealous of what they drive, where they live, what they wear, how they look, where they go out to eat, where they take their vacations, where they go to church, etc. You might not know how much God is blessing them. He will give you the desires of your heart. God doesn't spend time worrying about your wants, but He supplies all your needs! Do you truly worship Him? Do you give Him back the ten percent in tithes that He asks you for? These and many more questions can be asked over and over again. God sits high, but He looks low. He actually know what you are doing. If you praise and worship Him, He will truly bless you! We all have sinned and come short of the glory of Christ. But don't use this as an excuse to do sin after sin, because "God doesn't put no more on you than you can bear." Everything that He does is for your good.

Back when I was young, I would want the same clothes that my friends had. I would want them so bad that I would borrow them from my other friends. I would also do the same things that my friends did—good or bad. Whatever they did, I would do it, too. Now monkey see, monkey do.

But I also think back on growing up next to the basketball court at the Sunflower Elementary School in Sunflower, Mississippi. My mother used to fuss at us, my nephew and me, about trying to play on Sunday mornings. Coincidently, the church, Baptist Grove Church, was on the other side of the house. She told us that we could only play basketball when Sunday school was turned out. Now, this was the only time that I wouldn't try to do what my friends did. I knew my mom didn't play that! She told us that we must always put God first in our lives. Some of my friends started going to church with us on Sunday mornings. Now monkey see, monkey do.

Oh, what a wonderful this world this would be if everyone would worship God the same way! What we sometimes fail to realize is that God has no favorites. He loves all His children the same! He blesses you, the same as He blesses me. He loves you, the same as He loves me. He heals you from your illnesses, the same way He heals me. He protects you, the same way He protects me. He walks and talks with you, the same way He walks and talks to me.

To me, the Joneses can have anything that they want. All I want and need is Jesus! Oh, how I love Jesus! If you want to be like Jesus, now monkey see, monkey do! "Listen to my voice and follow my direction, and I will show you how to be successful in your family, your profession, and your finances. I take the greatest pleasure in seeing you prosper" (Deuteronomy 30:8-9, AMP). Thank God. Amen.

DO THINGS THAT ARE PLEASING TO GOD!

WHO ARE YOU?

We all need to look in the mirror and try to figure out,
What our lives are really all about.
What do you see when you take a look?
Is it someone out of your favorite story book?
Man sees your outside appearance,
But before you can go to Heaven, you will need to get clearance.
Are you a loser in life or are you winning?
Man has made a lot of mistakes, ever since the beginning.
Have you ever turned your back on a friend?
Now, this is one of your greatest sins.
Be the person God wants you to be,
Always keep your head up, and stand tall as a tree!
Try to keep bad thoughts out of your mind,
Because when you do right, you'll be around for a very long time!
So, I still ask, who are you?
Believe in God's promises and all your dreams will come true!
Stop trying to be like your neighbors and friends,
Live a life that will lead you to a pleasant end!

CHRISTMAS (2002)

Jesus Christ has and will always be "the reason for the season!" It's not about what someone gets you, what you may want, or what you might want to get someone else, but it's all about Jesus! Mary and Joseph were given the most beautiful and best gift that any parent can be proud of—the Savior of men. Just think, the shepherds came from all over the world to see this "King." He wasn't born in a hospital or clinic, like babies of today are born. He was born in a manger because there was no room in the inn. He was brought all kinds of gold, coins, rubies, and etc. He was truly worthy to be praised! We enjoy all comforts: heat, blanket, and beds. But, Baby Jesus had to sleep out in the cold of the night.

During this special time of the year, remember what our Savior had to endure from birth until His death for us. Take some time out of your busy schedule or life and do something good for someone who is less fortunate than yourself. You may think that you have it bad. You need to visit some of the homeless shelters, care-inns, prisons, hospitals, etc. You will just praise and thank God for all He has done for you! Lord, we truly thank you for giving us "the very best gift" any man or woman could ever receive, Jesus! Oh how I love Jesus!

During this holiday season and everyday, we lift up His holy name! It's all in your name, Lord! "And she shall bring forth a son, and thou shalt call His name Jesus; for He shall save His people from their sins." Matthew 1:21. KJV. We need to ask God to give us a "giving spirit," not just during this holiday season, but all year round. My prayer is for peace on Earth, and good will toward men. Merry Christmas and have a happy new year! Thank God. Amen.

HAPPY BIRTHDAY TO YOU, JESUS!

WHAT DOES CHRISTMAS MEAN TO ME?

Christmas is a special day of the year,
That everyone is filled with love and cheer.
Why should we wait until this day,
To love our family and friends in a special way.
We should spread our love all year through,
Instead of sitting around and feeling blue.
Jesus Christ wasn't born in something as comfortable as a house,
But in a stable where there were animals, and probably even a mouse.
How could you mistreat such a great king?
The wise men brought gold, silver, rubies, and rings.
Everyone gets into a giving mood,
No one is fighting or being rude.
I really hate to see this day come to an end,
When people take time out to love and respect their family and friends.
We need to love each other day in and day out,
It would stop us from worrying so much or having any doubt.
Christmas should be filled with joy and peace,
And love for our fellowman, now this is the way it supposed to be!

PART TWO

ARE YOU REALLY MY FRIEND?

Friends, how many of us truly have them? How many do we really need? These are just a few of the questions that continue to puzzle my mind, day in and day out. The friend I am talking about is one who would lay down his or her life, so that I may live. Not someone that gives me a ride when my car breaks down, calls and gives me a word of sympathy when someone close to me dies, gives me advice when I am faced with a problem, talks to me when he or she wants something, and I go out with from time to time. The friend that I need is there from the beginning and stay until my end. He will never leave me nor forsake me, even when men criticize me.

The friend that I am talking about is Jesus. "Greater love hath man than this, that man lay down his life for his friends" (John 15:13, KJV). Whenever I get lonely, depressed, need someone to talk to, or need financial counseling, I just call on Jesus. Just think, what kind of man would sacrifice his own life to save someone else? We all need to think long and hard about this, would we really do this? When a fireman or policeman risks his or her life to save someone, we say that he or she was only doing his or her job. But we never think that these people may actually be Christians. They may have taken an oath, not just for the city, but also with God. They may have decided to save us from hurt, harm, or danger. You know, most people consider these people as "heroes," but God considers them as "friends." Just think about it, they laid down their lives to save others!

"God sent his son Jesus to pay the price for our sins. He loved us so much; He was willing to take our punishment for being unable to keep all His commands. When we put our trust in him as our Savior, God's spirit comes to dwell in our hearts, and God blesses us in the same way he blessed Abraham" (Galatians 3:13-14, AMP). So, after all that, are you really my friend? It's hard to compare to Jesus, for no man gets to the Father, except through the Son. Let's all pray that we can be friends! I love you and lift up the name of the Lord! Thank God. Amen.

45

WHERE ARE ALL MY FRIENDS?

I think often of my friends from long ago,
Where are they now, I do not know.
But one friend has been there from the very start,
He is the one who is the most dearest and closest to my heart!
His name is Jesus, God's son,
He was sent to deliver us from the "Evil One."
Jesus is my real "friend,"
He will be there for me until the very end.
Friends may come, and friends may go,
But this is one friend that I have really gotten to know.
He has been around me when I was glad,
He lifted me back up when I was feeling sad.
I have love for Him since I was very young,
No one in this world knows where He has delivered me from!

GOD IS WATCHING YOU

Remember the song, "I Always Feel Like Somebody's Watching Me"? You know that everywhere you go somebody is watching you no matter where you may go. That somebody that I am referring to is God. We may try to hide things we do from our spouse, mother, father, sister, brother, friends, etc. But, you know, you can't hide from God. He's always watching. Our God sits high, but he looks low. He knows what each and everyone of us is doing. God is the shepherd of His flock and keeps us from hurt, harm, or danger. "For He shall give His angels charge over thee, to keep thee in all thy ways" (Psalms 91:11, KJV).

All day and all night, I know an angel is watching over me! We must always remember that God is in control of all our lives. Just imagine that God has one of the largest big screen television that you have ever seen. He has total control over each and every channel with a very large remote control. He's able to adjust the picture, focus, language, short play, long play, extended play, slow play, record, rewind, and etc. I know that God makes the right decision about all our lives. He makes no mistakes! Everything that happens to us happens for a reason! "I will instruct you and teach you in the way you should go. I will counsel you and watch over you" (Psalms 32:8, AMP).

So whenever you think that you're all alone, just look up towards Heaven and remember, God is watching you. "Your ears shall hear a word behind you saying, this is the way, walk in it, when you turn to the right hand and when you turn to the left" (Isaiah 30:21, AMP).

I have my personal testimony on how God is watching you. On April 15, 2002, I had just come from our male chorus rehearsal at New Life Baptist Church. We had been rehearsing for a "Men's Day" program at the church. I had made it home with no complications. I felt great! I began coughing and needed a drink of water. I went to get a drink from the sink. I fell to the floor and began to choke. I was having a seizure. I tried to make some kind of noise

47

to alert my family. My family was asleep and couldn't hear a thing. Our dog didn't even make a sound. I tried to call my wife's name, but I couldn't utter a sound. I passed out and didn't see anything but total darkness. I finally thought to call on the Lord, but I found out that He was there all the time. I felt my body being lifted up from the floor and back on my feet. I was choking to death, but now I felt a breath of fresh air in my lungs. I felt a spirit present. Thank you, Lord! He spared my life! He gave me a second chance! I love the Lord with all my heart and soul! Thank God! Amen!

I AM SO GLAD GOD WATCHES OVER ME

THE SPECIAL SOMEONE

No matter what's going on or what you have to do,
God is always there for you.
He is my Heavenly Father and best friend,
I will love Him to the very end!
He is ever present in my life,
He has truly helped me through a lot of heartaches, pains, and strife.
He has been there for me from the very start,
He is very special to me and I love Him with all my heart!
I've been up and I've been down,
One thing I can say is that I have never been seen with a frown.
Whenever I feel all alone,
I know I don't have to call Him on the telephone.
I pray to God to bless His best friend,
And to give Him strength to endure to the end!
So, if I don't live to see another day again,
I will always remember that God will get us all together:
My father, mother, brothers, sisters, family, and friends!

TURN OUT THE LIGHTS, THE PARTY IS OVER

You know that we have some so-called Christians out there that still think that life is a party. They think that they are still able to run with the "big dogs." Some even go out partying with their children. Just think, how can you tell your child to come home at a decent time on Saturday night when you are there to close the nightclub up? Then you have the audacity to tell them that they should get up early for Sunday school, while you are still in the bed. You can't even get out of the bed yourself. We need to get control of our lives.

"I'm in love with Mary Jane, she is my main thang, she makes me feel alright, she makes my heart sang, and when I'm feeling low, she comes as no surprise, she will spread her love, and take me to paradise!" You know, Mary Jane is marijuana. But let me tell you what God is like compared to marijuana or crack cocaine. Once you get Him into your system, you can't get enough of Him. You will inhale His words and don't want to exhale. God will take you higher than you have ever been! First time: you'll never experience anything like Him. Second time: you'll tell your family and friends about Him. Third time: your life starts changing. Fourth time: you just can't get enough of Him. Fifth time: things start to happen that you can't explain. Sixth time: you love Him with all your heart and soul. Seventh time: you will want to spend all your time with Him and on and on.

I'm reminded of the time when Moses took the slaves of Egypt into the Promised Land. Moses went into the mountains to pray and worship to God. The people were of little faith, believing that Moses had deserted them, and were talked into worshiping other gods and "partying." Moses returned with the Ten Commandments. The party was destroyed and some of the people. A question was asked, "Who's on the Lord's side?" I was once told by an elder that you should live every day like it's your last!

But He was wounded for our transgressions, He was bruised for our iniquities: the chastisement of our peace was upon Him: and with His stripes we are healed. "All we like sheep have gone astray: we have turned everyone

51

to His own way: and the Lord hath laid on Him the iniquities of us all" (Isaiah 53:5-6, KJV). Thank God. Amen.

OBEY THE COMMANDMENTS OF GOD,
AND THERE WILL BE ETERNAL LIFE!

GOING HOME

I'm reminded of *The Wizard of Oz*, one of my favorite childhood books, when I think about "going home." All Dorothy wanted to do was go home, and home was back to her family in Kansas. She had to endure a lot of trials and tribulations, and take a lot of journeys through unkind areas. She faced many circumstances and trouble—even death—on every corner. Everyone told her that she needed to see the Wizard, he would be the only one that could get her back home. She found out that a lot of other people needed to see the Wizard also. They had things that the Wizard needed to do for them too. (Now put God in the place of the wizard, and think about your situation.)

I remember when my mother was on her sick bed. She came to me in my sleep, about a few days before she died. She told me, "I'm going home, son." I questioned my mother, but I couldn't get an answer. So, after a few days, my mother passed. All she wanted me to know was that she was leaving her old earthly home and going to live in Heaven. We know not how long we will be here, but we know one day we will all leave here! But, in order for us to go our Heavenly Home, we have to get to know Jesus! Don't get me wrong, I love my earthly home, but I want to move much higher, right up there on 111 Holy Ghost Drive.

The hardest thing for us to do is leave home. But at the end of our journey, we all are "going home." "Come to me, all you who are weary and burdened, and I will give you rest. Take my yoke upon you and learn from me, for I am gentle and humble in heart, and you will find rest for your soul" (Matthew 11:28-29, AMP). A lot of people want to go to heaven and live in a mansion, but not me. I will be happy just to live in a shack! Just to be in the presence of the Lord will be good enough for me! We know not "the time nor the hour in which the Lord will come," so we all know that we must be ready!

"I am your provider and protector. Because you put your trust in me, I will meet all your needs. Though you walk through the midst of trouble, do not be afraid, because I am always with you. I will guide you and keep you from harm. My mercy and goodness will surround you, and you will have a 'home' with me forever" (Psalms 23:1,2,6, AMP). Thank God. Amen.

IN ORDER FOR US TO GO HOME,
WE MUST GET TO KNOW JESUS!

THERE'S NO PLACE LIKE HOME

Home is a place where I love to go,
It's a place of contentment and peace, you know.
The home that I am talking about is built with love,
And it is blessed by the "One Above."
Home is where the heart is,
I know this is where Jesus lives.
I wouldn't expect anything less,
Then to live for God and do my very best!
I've dreamed about living in the perfect atmosphere,
But I know it's nowhere on Earth or around here.
I've been everywhere and can't seem to find that perfect place,
Where everyone doesn't discriminate against you about your color,
religion, or race.
One thing that I have learned during the times when I roamed,
That there is no place like home!

GONE BUT NOT FORGOTTEN

This is what is put on the tombstone when we are gone from this world, but is this saying really true? Sometimes, we have to take into account of our lives on Earth. Do I love my neighbors, enemies, friends, and family as I love myself? You should give them the flowers as they yet live, so they can smell them and see them, and they know that you love them! It is not too much to let that person know that you love them. I hope and pray that when I'm gone, I'm not forgotten. I want everyone to remember that McKinley Cooper Jr. helped at least one person along the way. I might have given them an encouraging word, sang a song, prayed a prayer, gave someone a ride, a helping hand, saved someone's life, listened to someone else's problems, and gave them the right advice with the help of the Lord. I want to leave a memory of myself in someone's heart and mind forever! Through God all things are possible, if you only believe! "My son, attend to my words, consent, and submit to my sayings, let them not depart from your sight, keep them in the center of your heart" (Proverbs 4:20-21, KJV). Some people that are gone have been forgotten.

When you have a bad attitude toward your brothers and sisters, do you think that they will keep the memory of you in their hearts? Try to get along with everyone! Show them love and respect while you yet live. Be good to all people, friends, and enemies too. Try to live a life that is pleasing to God. Do good deeds, help the poor, encourage others to be closer to God, and most of all, do God's will.

It's bad when no one even thinks about you when you are gone. Give the people that know you something good to say about you when you are gone. "They that sow in tears shall reap in joy. He that goeth forth and weepeth, bearing precious seed, shall doubtless come again with rejoicing, bringing his sheaves with him" (Psalm 126:5-6, KJV). Thank God. Amen.

IS THIS SAYING REALLY TRUE?

DON'T FORGET YOUR PAST
(A TRIBUTE TO BLACK HISTORY)

I think a lot about our ancestors from the past,
They proved to us that our trials are just a test, and they will not last.
We sometimes forget how they were abused,
Our right to vote was greatly refused.
Some lost their lives just to set us free,
They were drowned with water, shot, burned, and hung from a tree.
When I think about this, it makes me sad,
Why people would treat another race so bad.
Jesus Christ died for all our sins,
He didn't see a particular race or color, but he considered us all "his
friends!"
I pray to God to show us all one day,
How to love all our brothers and sisters the same way.
Now this is a "new day," don't dwell in the past,
Always remember, those trials were just a test, and we are living proof that
they did not last!

LOST SOULS

We all go through life longing to be a Christian. We sometimes fail to realize that it's not what people think about us, but what God thinks. We sometimes look for guidance in all the wrong places. God shows and tells us the way that we should go, if we would only take the time to listen and look. Sometimes He uses other people to minister to us, just to let us know that He's giving us the answer. God has made an agenda for each and every one of us to follow. For God is truly in charge of your life! No matter the situation or circumstance, He is truly worthy to be praised! All you have to do is ask Him for forgiveness of all your sins, and He will do it.

I was once "lost," but now I have been found, only by His grace and mercy! God knows that while you are looking and searching, He has already found you. Praise His holy name! One thing that I learned on my Christian journey is that He may not show up when you want Him too, but He's always "on time!" "Change your life by meditating on my word. Then you will understand and be certain of my will for every area of your life" (Romans 12:2, AMP).

You know, when your soul is lost, it's similar to being blind. Someone has to lead you because you can't see how to do things for yourself. This situation relates to religion. If your leader tells you what thus saith the Lord, but he does totally opposite, then he too has a lost soul. You should pray to God to give Him guidance and understanding to help His flock. You, in turn, have been given five senses from God. You need to know right from wrong for yourself. Man perishes every day because of lack of knowledge about God. He will lead and direct us in the path He wants us to walk and follow in. Just believe and have faith that God will step in. " I will instruct thee and teach thee in the way which thou shalt go: I will guide thee with mine eye" (Psalms 32:8, KJV). Thank God. Amen.

I WAS ONCE LOST, BUT NOW I AM FOUND!

MOTHER'S DAY (2002)

In forty years, this is the first time that I won't have a living mother to tell "Happy Mother's Day" to. I really miss my mother a whole lot. If you haven't experienced life without a mother, you don't know what I really mean or feel. After all the pain and frustration of waking up this morning, I still thank God for this day.

But I can still remember that Tuesday morning around at 3:00 a.m. We were sitting on the bank of the river fishing. (Oh, how my mother loved to fish!) We would fish from sunrise to sunset! I tried to talk to her, but when I tried to, God would speak to me. He told me to get the flowers and fence that I had thought about getting, and to go to Sunflower, Mississippi, and put them on my mother's grave. I knew that it had to be God, because only my wife knew what I wanted to do. As the time passed by, I glanced at the clock for a brief moment. I saw that it was now 4:00 a.m. I told God that I needed some sleep, because I needed to get up for work in a couple of hours. But, God said to me, "My son, I can give you a couple of hours of sleep and make it seem like a day." I started to laugh, because I thought even God has a sense of humor! He told me that Mom was with Him now, and that she was fine. He wanted me to tell the family that the only way we would see her again is that we would get ourselves right with Him.

So, I went to work that day and felt no-ways tired! God will truly do what He say He will do! I also asked the Lord what I needed to sing on Mother's Day at my church. "On That Other Shore" wasn't the one, because he wasn't ready for me to come to the other shore yet. "Hide Behind the Mountain" wasn't the one, because this was my personal testimony. I know Him for myself and what He has done for me. "Stay on the Line" was the one of choice! No matter what you have been going through, God will bring you out! Choir rehearsal was also on that Tuesday night. On Saturday, I didn't have any idea about what would actually happen. I picked up the fence and the flowers on our way to Sunflower, Mississippi. When my family made it to town, it was around 3:00 p.m. My family in Sunflower was glad to see us. One of my sisters told me that they had planned to go to the cemetery and put flowers on our mother's grave for Mother's Day at 4:00 p.m.. Call it luck, coincidence, or whatever you want to, but I call it an act of God.

God is real because I can feel Him in my soul! They didn't even let me know what they had planned . I hadn't been out the hospital more than a couple of weeks, after being diagnosed with congestive heart failure. My sisters, four from Mississippi and one from Chicago, were there. Some of my nieces and their families, some nephews, (one from Atlanta that had missed my mother's funeral) were also there. One of my nieces from Jackson, Mississippi, had brought me a get-well card for my sister to send me.

I told the family at the cemetery about the vision that God had given me, and also what He told me to tell them. "Do not become discouraged! Your situation may seem impossible in the natural, but if you put your hope in Me, I am able to change your circumstances. Nothing is impossible, if you only 'believe'" (Mark 9:23, AMP).

We left that Saturday evening to return to Memphis. I thought about what had happened on that special day. I will truly never forget it!

I woke up that Sunday morning (Mother's Day), and thanked God! I went to church and had a good time in the Lord! I wished my mother a "Happy Mother's Day," and told her that I loved her! I was left with this thought about my mom: "Everyone will see how I have blessed your life. I will give you abundant prosperity and I will bless the work of your hands. You will be the lender and not the borrower. I will make you a leader and not a follower. You will be a success and not a failure. This is the plan I have for you my child, so choose a life of obedience and I will bring it to pass all that I have promised" (Deuteronomy 28:1-3, AMP). Thank God. Amen.

HAPPY MOTHER'S DAY TO MOTHERS EVERYWHERE

LETTING GO
(A POEM FOR MY MOTHER)

You know it's very hard to let go
Of the person you hold dear to you and know.
When I cried, she wiped away my tears,
And when I was afraid, she calmed my fears.
I thank God for putting me into her life,
He made her so sweet and nice.
She had been around me for a very long time,
I know God will always keep her in my heart and mind.
I have missed her for quite a while,
I can no longer see her pretty smile.
Over the years, we had a lot of fun,
Fishing, talking, and enjoying the heat of the hot sun.
Now don't you realize why it's so hard for me to let go?
I know one day I will be able to tell her so.

MY THOUGHT ON 9/11/01

This was a wake-up call for everyone in the United States of America, including myself! Tomorrow is not promised for any of us. We all need to focus on today. You never know when will be the last time you get up in the morning, go to work or school, and lay down in your bed at night. That's why we need to praise God day and night, because we never know when we might leave this world. We have no idea on how we will spend our last day on Earth.

When I think about what took place, I'm reminded of the movie, *Left Behind*. Do all that you can to serve the Lord here on Earth, so that you can go to a better place! You know, I was afraid to die, because I didn't know what was beyond the sky. We all need to take an inventory of our lives and straighten out the things that we have messed up.

I hope and pray that the people who lost their lives went to a better place! "But no weapon that is formed against you shall prosper, and every tongue that shall rise against you in judgment you shall show to be in the wrong. This (peace, righteousness, security, triumph over opposition) is the heritage of the servants of the Lord" (Isaiah 54:17, AMP).

God has a plan for each and every one of us to follow. We all need to take time out of our busy lives to praise the Lord! Oh, how I love Jesus! We saw fireman and policeman that lay down their lives to save other people. All the U.S. citizens came together, united as one! Everyone's attention was drawn to New York: tears of sorrow, prayers of peace, and love for our fellow man! Now that's what it's all about! This is the love that God wants us to have towards one another, brotherly love!

If you haven't started praising the Lord by now, there may not ever be another tomorrow! "Because you have made the Lord your Refuge, and the Most High your dwelling place, there shall no evil befall you, nor any calamity come near your tent. For He will give His angels (especially) charge over you, to accompany and defend and preserve you in all your ways" (Psalms 91:9-11, AMP). Thank you, Lord. Amen.

GOD BLESS AMERICA. AMERICA, PRAISE GOD!

FEAR

Fear is one of the greatest emotions known to man,
It is one that I think is the hardest to understand.
When I think about it, I feel a lot of sorrow,
I sometimes ask myself, "Will I see tomorrow?"
Fear has been inside me for quite some time,
It is buried deep inside your mind.
I think a lot about the days when I was young,
I was afraid of the dark and the heat from the sun.
But God helps us through the thought of being scared,
Now what would you do if you ended up in Hell?
When I lay down to go to sleep,
If I should die, I pray to God my soul to keep.
I wonder what would I do if I lost my sight?
Would I walk around, like stumbling in the night?
I no longer fear anything when I walk out my door,
I truly thank God that I'm not afraid anymore!

LIVE FOR TODAY BECAUSE TOMORROW IS NOT PROMISED

What if you didn't wake up tomorrow morning? Where would you end up going to, Heaven or Hell? What if the alarm clock never went off, and no one was around to wake you up? What if the sun never rose the next morning? What if the telephone didn't ring tomorrow morning? These questions can easily be answered by telling yourself to live for today, and let God handle all your tomorrows. (I am talking about myself, too.)

We need to put on the "whole armour of God" today to protect us for tomorrow. We could leave our homes in our automobiles and have an accident that could take our lives; go to sleep and never wake up; get robbed and killed; or your home could burn up with you in it. There are a lot of possibilities, but a serious prayer to God each and every day is the only solution to the problem. We must learn to live our lives one day at a time, an hour at a time, a minute at a time, and even a second at a time. We should pray to God to give us the strength to endure until the end.

I find myself wondering if I will see tomorrow. I have already had the experience of not being able to see tomorrow . I could have been dead and sleeping in my grave, but God wasn't quite ready for me. He gave me a second chance to get my "house" in order. I thank Him every day to see another day: rain, sleet, snow, or hail! "Today is another day that the Lord has made, so let us rejoice and be glad in it" (Psalms 118:24, KJV).

But if I didn't wake up tomorrow morning, I know that I'm in your hands, Lord! Because life and death is in God's Hands! If you're putting away your savings for tomorrow, tell someone where the money is, you may not be here to spend it.

I get tired sometimes, but I know one day God will give me eternal rest. "Look, today I have set before you life and death, depending on whether you obey or disobey...I call Heaven and Earth to witness you that today I have set before you life, or death, blessing or curse. Oh that you would choose life; that you and your children might live" (Deuteronomy 30:15,19, AMP).

67

Through God, all things are possible! God has a plan for each and every one of us to follow. He knows when you won't see tomorrow! I was once told by my mother to "never put off today for tomorrow may never come!"

AS FOR ME, I'M LETTING GOD DECIDE
WHEN I WON'T SEE TOMORROW

TIME WAITS ON NO ONE

It's funny how many years have gone by,
Some have made you laugh, and some have made you cry.
You know, that's when God shows up in your life,
He helps you through all the heartaches, pains, and strife!
Time waits on no one, and is always in a hurry,
Then why waste it and sit around and worry!
Enjoy the good times and pray about the bad,
For some of us, they may be the best years that we may have ever had!
Think back on the years when you were young,
You laughed and joked, and had a lot of fun.
The time has gone by so fast,
The bad times that you had, should be left in the past!

LET GO/LET GOD

No matter the circumstance or the situation, God is always there to bring you out of any situation! Just call on His holy name, and He will bring you out!

I know from experience that if you ask Him for something, He may not give it to you when you want Him too, but it is always on time! It only takes faith the size of a mustard seed! Don't give up, because the battle isn't yours, it's the Lord! But, if you truly believe upon Him, you won't even have to worry. He is there and always will be there! There is nothing that God can't handle!

"I am your Heavenly Father and I always speak the truth. I know the purpose of your life so don't be discouraged when something you were hoping for doesn't occur. When the time is right, I will open a door for you, and no man will be able to close it" (Revelations 3:7-8, AMP).

We think that we can take care of our own problems or situation, and don't need anyone's help. We must realize that God is the only help we need! He is in the hospitals, prisons, on our jobs, in the schools, in our homes, on the highways, in foreign countries, etc. God is everywhere, we have Him in our hearts and minds.

"Rejoice, as you put your faith in Me, knowing that I will defend you. Let your heart fill with joy, realizing how I desire to bless your life. I will surround you with people who highly respect and esteem you" Psalms 5:11-12,AMP).

Remember, God puts no more on us that we can't bear. That's why we must "Let go and let God do it for us!"

Thank God, Amen.

GOD PUTS US THROUGH SOME THINGS,
JUST TO BRING US BACK OUT!

AM I GIVING GOD MY ALL?

I often ask myself this question when I'm meditating on God's goodness. Am I good enough or have done anything that's worthy enough of God's grace and mercy? For God sent His Son to die for all of my sins. What have I done for Him lately? God has done so much for me, how can I ever repay Him? It would take a life time of worship and praise to repay Him!

He woke me up this morning from my sleep. He started me on my way. He made my trip to work safe. He helped me to make it through the work day. He made my trip home safe. I was able to do my work around the house . He blesses my food that is prepared for dinner. He lets me enjoy the time I spend with my family. He puts everything else from today out of my mind as I meditate on His words and Him. He prepares my mind and body for a good night's sleep. Now I ask you who couldn't serve a God like Him? He's my all-in-all! He is truly Alpha and Omega! All that He wants in return is for us to praise and worship Him. I thank Him daily for giving me a second chance on life. You know, He is the God of Second Chances! "Be humble by realizing that life is significant (James 4:10, AMP).

There will come a time in every man's life when he will have to give God his all-in-all! Don't wait until something happens in your life, but give Him the glory and honor right now, for He is truly worthy to be praised!

"Delight thyself also in the Lord; and He shall give thee the desires of thine heart. Commit thy way unto the Lord; trust also in Him ; He shall bring it to pass" (Psalm32:4-5). Thank you, Lord. Amen.

IT'S NEVER TOO LATE TO GIVE GOD YOUR ALL-IN -ALL!

LOVE

It is one of the greatest emotions that you will experience in the world,
It is one felt by every man, woman, boy, and girl!
I have always felt it, but have seldom said,
Some people don't say it, until you are dead.
So, I asked the Lord to help me'out,
He said, "Son, this word should make you shout!"
Just think about all the ones who cared for you,
When you were down and out, and feeling blue.
When your life was sinking into sin,
It was love that brought you out, to start all over again!
If you truly believe in Him, your "new life" begins!
It is a feeling that has been all around for a very long time,
I thank God for putting it into my mind!
Love is a word that is special to me,
Without love, I sometimes wonder where would I be?
I thank God for this word today,
Because I know He's capable of making a way!

THANKSGIVING DAY (2002)

I first I thank you, Lord, for letting your Son die on the cross for all our sins, so that we may live! I also thank you for giving me a father and a mother who were my soul providers; my wife, who is the mother of my child and love of my life; my job; my home; food on the table; and my life.

Weeping may endure for night, but I know that joy will come in the morning! Every day is the day of Thanksgiving because God has been so good to me! He has been there during my good times, and especially during the bad times! I know that He has dispatched Angels to watch over my family and me! I have been through the storms and the rain, heartaches and pain. I know that God was with me because when I felt like giving up, it was then that He carried me.

I owe Him so much, how can I ever repay Him? He just keep on giving, and giving, and giving, even when I don't ask Him for anything. Now, who wouldn't serve such a great God? I owe Him my life, and I have promised Him to do His will. One day I will get a chance to meet Him and tell Him how much I love Him!

Not only today, but every day, I salute You and praise your holy name! For you are truly worthy to be praised! For those of you who don't know Him, you need to get to know Him! He is my all-in-all, bridge over troubled waters, my sword and shield, my provider, my healer, my protector, my guide, my father and mother, my way maker, etc.

Some people only give thanks on Thanksgiving Day, the holiday set aside to give thanks, but this day exists when you get up in the morning to see another day! Families come together to celebrate this special occasion, which is good, but families should worship and fellowship together 365 days a year!

"This is another day that the Lord has made, let us rejoice and be glad in it" (Psalms 118:24, KJV). Just think about it, some of your love ones and friends didn't live to see this day. Just be thankful you're still here! "When they saw Him, they worshipped Him; but some doubted, and Jesus came and said unto them, 'All authority both in Heaven and on the Earth has been given to Me….and remember I am with you always, even to the ends of the Earth'" (Matthew 28:17-18, 28, KJV). Thank you, Lord. Amen

IT'S ALL ABOUT JESUS!

THANK YOU

These are two words that can be expressed with love,
They were created from the "One Above."
I can't begin to tell You how much YOU have blessed me.
Your acts of kindness stand out as tall as a tree!
I pray that You will bless me throughout the years,
I thank You so much that my face is filled with tears.
I will forever praise You in my prayers,
May You continue to bless me and watch over me,
and have a place for me up there!

WHAT DO I PRAY FOR?

We all go through life wondering what to ask God for. Some people only pray in the church because it makes them feel important. God tells us to humble ourselves and do this in connection with Him. Don't be selfish and only pray for yourself. Pray for other people, too. If things aren't going right in your home, pray for the entire family. If things aren't going right on your job, pray for the whole company. If things aren't going right in the schools, pray for the whole school system, etc. The battle isn't yours, it's the Lord's! Take all your problems to Him, He'll work it out!

Sometimes we have to go inside our secret closet and just have a talk with God. The most important thing to happen to you is when your prayers are answered. Sometimes, God will send a perfect stranger to you to confirm your situation and tell you what thus said the Lord. "I call on you, O God, for you will answer me; give ear to me and hear my prayer. Show the wonder of your greatest love, you who save by your right hand, those who take refuge in you from their foes. Keep me as the apple of your eye; hide me in the shadows of your wing" (Psalms 17: 6-8, AMP).

God instructs other people to come to you or to pray for you. Don't wait until something bad happens to you or your loved ones to pray. We need to bray both in and out of seasons! Whenever we need help, prayer is the right thing to do. We can tell God the situation, and have faith that He will answer your prayer. It will happen exactly at the right time!

I pray that God will deliver some of my family members from drugs, alcohol, sickness and disease, personal problems, lost of a loved one, etc. Prayer is a one-on-one communication between you and God. Just remember that everything works together for the good to those who love God! "Don't worry about anything; instead pray about everything; tell God your needs, and don't forget to thank Him for His answers. If you do this, you will experience God's peace, which is far more wonderful than the human mind can understand. His peace will keep your thoughts and your heart quiet and at rest as you trust in Jesus Christ" (Philippians 4:6-7, AMP). Thank God. Amen.

PRAYER IS THE KEY AND FAITH UNLOCKS THE DOOR!

GOING HOME

Sometimes I really feel confused,
Jesus Christ still died for our sins, even after He was abused!
Why should we have to go through so many disappointments in life?
If it wasn't for the Lord, I would feel stabbed in the back by a knife!
You know it gets hard to run this old race,
I know one day I will leave this place!
I will really miss my family and my friends,
I hope and pray that one day I will see them again!
One thing that I can say is that it has been a great life,
I have filled it with all the love and joy of Jesus Christ!
I don't want anyone close to me to feel sad,
Because when I go away, I will be at a place where I will always be glad!

VISIONS

My first vision came to me before my mother's death. I saw her for the last time that night. She told me that she was "going home," and I wondered what she was talking about. I opened my eyes to see where she was. She was in a coffin and I now knew what she was talking about! I heard music playing in the background about going to a better home in the sky. I couldn't tell anyone—not even my wife—about what I had seen that night. One thing, I didn't know if this vision was true.

After a few days had passed, my mom died. God was really trying to prepare me for the loss because He knew how much I loved my mother. When I went back home, and I saw her in the coffin at the funeral home, I almost fell apart. It was just like I remembered seeing her in my vision. But, as usual, God brought me through it all! This vision happened in January, 2002.

The next vision came to me in April, 2002. I was sitting on the couch in the den one Monday night. I started coughing and went to the kitchen to get a drink of water. I fell to the floor and began to have a seizure. I pounded my face into the floor until I passed out. I was in total darkness and couldn't see anything. I saw a light and was told to get in it. I tried to wake my family up, but I couldn't make a sound. I called on the Lord, but He was present all the time. I felt a breath of fresh air fill my lungs. I felt myself being lifted back up, but it was a spirit. I went to the doctor's office early the next morning. The doctor kept on asking me how I felt. I told him that I felt good, except for a little soreness in my chest and neck. He told me that according to the tests that he ran on me, at some point during the night, my heart had stopped beating. I couldn't tell him how long that I had been out and he couldn't either. He told me that I was suffering from a mild concussion, too. I was transported by ambulance to Baptist East Hospital, after being diagnosed with congestive heart failure, and placed in the intensive care unit in the hospital.

Another vision came during Mother's Day, 2002. I saw my mother again, but this time we were on the bank of the river fishing. I thought that we were alone, but there was someone in the background talking to me. God was present! He told me that my mom was doing fine now. He told me not to worry about her because she was with Him now, and the only way that any of the family would see her again, is that we would get right with Him. He told me to get the flowers and fence that I had thought about getting, and to go to Sunflower, Mississippi, and put them on my mother's grave. After I went down there most of the family had decided to get together and put flowers on her grave for the Mother's Day. No one had even called me about what they had decided to do. God is truly good all the time. I was so thankful to God for letting me see my mother again, and that she was all right! "If you abide in me, and my words abide in you, ye shall ask what ye will, and it shall be done unto you" (John 15:7, KJV).

I have a lot of other visions that the Lord has given to me to share with no one else. They are real, and only God knows His plans for my life. I also remember Him telling me that some will believe you, and some will doubt you, just as they did my son Jesus. "Delight thyself also in the Lord; and He shall give thee desires of thine heart. Commit thy way unto the Lord; trust also in Him; and He shall bring it to pass" (Psalms 37:4-5, KJV). Thank you, Lord. Amen.

THANK YOU, LORD, FOR GIVING ME THE POWER TO SEE THINGS IN THE FORM OF VISIONS!

AM I DREAMING?

Dreams do come true,
All you have to do is believe in "you."
God started it all for me,
When He gave His Son's life to set me free.
Sometimes I think that I'm not so worthy,
Then God tells me to leave everything alone and not to worry.
Anything that I need, He gives to me,
Why shouldn't I just stand still, like a tree?
God has a plan for all of us,
We don't have to fight or fuss.
Your breakthrough will come at the right time,
All you have to do is keep God in your heart and mind.
So, am I dreaming, or is this vision real?
I'm still living, healthy, and have been happy for the last two years!

Printed in the United States
28105LVS00005B/325-393